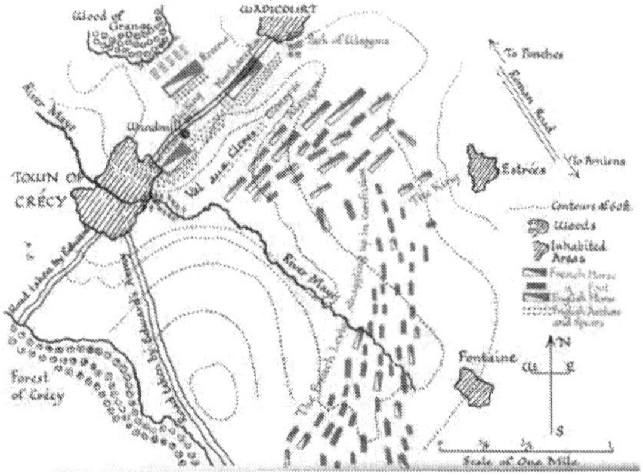

Crécy

Hilaire Belloc

Originally Published by

Stephen Swift and Co., Ltd.
1912

Contents

INTRODUCTION

Between those last precise accounts of military engagements which antiquity has left us in small number, and what may be called the modern history of war, there lies a period of many centuries—quite 1400 years—during which the details of an action and even the main features of a campaign are never given us by contemporary recorders.

Through all that vast stretch of time we are compelled, if we desire to describe with any accuracy, and at any length, the conduct of a battle, to "reconstitute" the same. In other words, we have to argue from known conditions to unknown. We have to establish by a comparison of texts and of traditions, and by other processes which will be dealt with in a moment, a number of elements which, where a modern action is concerned, numerous memoirs and official record often accompanied by elaborate maps can put clearly before us.

We should note that the line of division between what we will call a medieval battle and a modern one, though it cannot, of course, be precisely established, corresponds roughly to the sixteenth century. The battles of the seventeenth are for the most part open in detail to the historian, from copious evidence afforded by contemporary writers and by our considerable knowledge of the tactics and armament of the time. And this, of course, is still truer of the eighteenth and of the nineteenth centuries. Subsequent to the wide employment of printing, and throughout the sixteenth century, the tendency shown by contemporaries to set down detail steadily increases, but the whole of that century is transitional in this matter.

The battles of the fifteenth, of the fourteenth, and earlier centuries, differ entirely as to their evidence. We must gather it from manuscript authorities, often rare, sometimes unique. Those authorities are, again, not always contemporary. They never by any chance give us a map, and rarely a definite topographical indication. They are summary, their motive is ecclesiastical or civil rather than military, they present at the best the picturesque side of an engagement, and at the worst they preserve a bare mention of its date, or the mere fact that it took place.

Even in the elementary point of numbers, without some knowledge of which it is so difficult to judge the nature of a field, we are commonly at a loss. Where a smaller force upon the defensive has discomfited a larger attacking force, the dramatic character of such a success (and Crécy was one of them) has naturally led to an exaggeration of the disproportion. The estimate of loss is very commonly magnified and untrustworthy, for that is an element which, in the absence of exact record, both victors and vanquished inevitably tend to enlarge. We are not as a rule given the hours, sometimes, but not often, the state of the weather, and, especially in the earlier cases, the local or tactical result is of so much greater importance to the chronicler than the strategical plan, that we are left with little more knowledge at first hand than the fact that A won and B lost.

So true is this, that with regard to the majority of the great actions of the Dark Ages no contemporary record even enables us to fix their site within a few miles. That is true, for instance, of the decisive defeat of Attila in 451, of the Mahommedans by Charles Martel in 732, and of the final victory of Alfred over the Danes in 878.

Scholarship has established, with infinite pains and within small limits of doubt, the second and the third. The first is still disputed. So it is with the victory of Clovis over the Visigoths, and with any number of minor actions. Even when we come to the later centuries, and to a more complete knowledge, we are pursued by this difficulty, though it is reduced. Thus we know the square mile within which the Battle of Hastings was fought, but the best authorities have disputed its most important movements and characters. Similarly we can judge the general terrain of most of the Crusading fights, but with no precision, and only at great pains of comparison and collation.

The battle which forms the object of this little monograph, late as was its date, was long the subject of debate during the nineteenth century, upon the elementary point of the English position and its aspect. And, though that and other matters may now be regarded as established, we owe our measure of certitude upon them not to any care upon the part of our earliest informers, but to lengthy and close argument conducted in our time.

There is no space in such a short book as this to discuss all the causes which combined to produce this negligence of military detail in the medieval historian: that he was usually not a soldier, that after the ninth century armies cannot be regarded as professional, and that the interest of the time lay for the mass of readers in the results rather than in the action of a battle, are but a few of these.

But though we have no space for any full discussion, it is worth the reader's while to be informed of the general process by which scholarship attempts to reconstitute an engagement, upon which it has such insufficient testimony; and as the Battle of Crécy is the first in this series which challenges this sort of research, I will beg leave to sketch briefly the process by which it proceeds.

The first thing to be done, then, in attempting to discover what exactly happened during such a battle as that of Crécy, is to tabulate our sources. These are of three kinds—tradition, monuments, and documents.

Of these three, tradition is by far the most valuable in most research upon affairs of the Dark or Middle Ages, and it is nothing but a silly intellectual prejudice, the fruit of a narrow religious scepticism, now fast upon the wane, which has offered to neglect it.

Unfortunately, however, tradition is a particularly weak guide in this one department of knowledge. In estimating the character of a great man it is invaluable. It plays a great part in deciding us upon the nature of social movements, in helping us to locate the sites of buildings that have disappeared, and particularly of shrines; it gives us ample testimony (too often neglected) to the authenticity of sacred documents, and to the origin of laws. It is even of some assistance in establishing certain main points upon a military action, if documents are in default. For instance, a firm tradition of the site of a battle is evidence not only in the absence of documents, but in negation of doubtful or vague ones, and so is a firm tradition concerning the respective strength of the parties, if that tradition can be stated in general terms. But for the particular interest of military history it is worthless because it is silent. Even the civilian to-day, and, for that matter, the soldier as well, who is not accustomed to this science, would find it tedious to note, and often impossible to recognise, those points which form the salient matters for military history. There can be no tradition of the exact moments in which such and such a development in a battle occurred, of contours, of range, etc., save where here and there some very striking event (as in the case of the projectile launched into the midst of Acre during the Third Crusade) startles the mind of the onlooker, and remains unforgotten.

In the particular case of Crécy, tradition fixes for us only two points—though these have proved of considerable importance in modern discussion—the point where the King of Bohemia fell, and the point from which Edward III. watched the battle.

Of monuments, again, we have a very insufficient supply, and in the case of Crécy, hardly any, unless the point already alluded to, where the blind king was struck down, and the cross marking it be counted, as also the foundations of the mill, which was the view-point of the English commander.

It is to documents, then, that we must look, and, unfortunately for this action, our principal document is not contemporary. It is from the pen of Froissart, who was but nine years old when the battle was fought, and who wrote many years after its occurrence. Even so, his earlier version does not seem to be familiar to the public of this country, though it is certainly the more accurate.

Froissart used a contemporary document proceeding from the pen of one "John the Fair," a canon of Liége. Of the lesser authorities some are contemporary: notably Baker of Swynford, and Villani, who died shortly after the battle.

But the whole bulk of material at our disposal is pitifully small, and the greater part of what the reader will have set before him in what follows is the result of an expansion and criticism of the few details which writers of the period have bequeathed to us.

When the documentary evidence, contemporary, or as nearly contemporary as possible, has been tabulated, the historian of a medieval battle next proceeds to consider what may be called the "limiting circumstances" within which the action developed, and these have much more than a negative value. As he proceeds to examine and to compare them, they illuminate many a doubtful point and expand many an obscure allusion.

For instance, in the case of Crécy, we carefully consider the contours, upon the modern map, of a terrain which no considerable building operations or mining has disfigured. We mark the ascertainable point at which the Somme was crossed, and calculate the minimum time in which a host of the least size to which we can limit Edward's force could have marched from that to the various points mentioned in the approach to the battle-field. We ascertain the distance from the scene of action to the forest boundary. We argue from the original royal possession and subsequent conservation of that forest its permanent limits. We can even establish with some accuracy the direction of the wind, knowing how the armies marched, how the sun stood relative to the advancing force, and their impression of the storm that broke upon them. We calculate, within certain limits of error, the distance necessary for deployment. We argue from the known character of the armour and weapons employed certain details of the attack and defence. We mark what were certainly the ancient roads, and we measure the permanent obstacles afforded by the physical nature of the field.

I give these few points as examples only. They are multiplied indefinitely as one's study proceeds, and in the result a fairly accurate description of so famous, though so ill attested, an action as this of Crécy can be reconstituted.

With all this there remains a large margin which cannot be generally set down as certain, and which even in matters essential must be written tentatively, with such phrases as "it would seem," or "probably" to excuse it. But history is consoled by the reflection that all these gaps may be filled by further research or further discovery, and that each new effort of scholarship bridges one and then another.

As to the critical power by which each individual writer will decide between conflicting statements, or apparently irreconcilable conditions, this must be left to his own power of discrimination and to the reader's estimate of his ability to weigh evidence. He is in duty bound—as I have attempted to do very briefly in certain notes—to give the grounds of his decision, and, having done so, he admits his reader to be a judge over himself: with this warning, however, that historical judgment is based upon a vast accumulation of detail acquired in many fields besides those particularly under consideration, and that a competent historian generally claims an authority in his decisions superior to that reposing upon no more than a mere view of limited contemporary materials.

I THE POLITICAL CIRCUMSTANCES

The Battle of Crécy was the first important decisive action of what is called "The Hundred Years' War." This war figures in many history books as a continued struggle between two organised nations, "England" and "France." To present it in its true historical character it must be stated in far different terms.

The Hundred Years' War consisted in two groups of fighting widely distant in time and only connected by the fact that from first to last a Plantagenet king of England claimed the Crown of France against a Valois cousin. Of these two groups of fighting the first was conducted by Edward III., and covers about twenty years of his reign. It was magnificently successful in the field, and gave to the English story the names of *Crécy* and of *Poitiers*. So far as the main ostensible purpose of that first fighting was concerned, it was unsuccessful, for it did not result in placing Edward III. upon the French throne.

The second group of actions came fifty years later, and is remembered by the great name of *Agincourt*.

This latter part of the Hundred Years' War was conducted by Henry V., the great-grandson of Edward III. and the son of the Lancastrian usurper. And Henry was successful, not only in the tactical results of his battles, but in obtaining the Crown of France for his house. After his death his success crumbled away; and a generation or so after Agincourt, rather more than one hundred years after the beginning of this long series of fights, the power of the kings of England upon the Continent had disappeared. As a visible result of all their efforts, nothing remained but the important bastion of Calais, the capture of which was among the earliest results of their invasions.

When we say that the ostensible object of all this conflict from first to last was the establishment of the Plantagenet kings of England as kings of France in the place of their cousins the Valois, we must remember what was meant by those terms in the fourteenth century, when Edward first engaged in the duel. There was no conception of the conquest of a *foreign* power such as would lie in the mind of a statesman of to-day. Society was still feudal. Allegiance lay from a man to his lord, not from a man to his central political government. Not only the religion, the thoughts, and the daily conduct of either party to the war were the same, but in the governing society of both camps the language and the very blood were the same. Edward was a Plantagenet. That is, his family tradition was that of one of the great French feudal nobles. It was little more than one hundred years before that his great-grandfather had been the actual and ruling Lord of Normandy, and of France to the west and the south-west, for the first Plantagenet, had though holding of the Crown at Paris, been the active monarch of Aquitaine, of Brittany, of Anjou, Normandy, and Maine.

So much for the general sentiment under which the war was engaged. As to its particular excuse, this was slight and hardly tenable, and we may doubt whether Edward intended to press it seriously. He engaged in the war from that spirit of chivalric adventure (a little unreal, but informed by an indubitable taste for arms) which was the mark of the fourteenth century, and which was at the same time a decline from the sincere knightly spirit of the thirteenth.

The excuse given was this. The French monarchy had descended, from its foundation in 987 right down to the death of Charles IV. in 1328, directly from father to son, but in that year, 1328, male issue failed the direct line. The obviously rightful claimant to the throne, according to the ideas of those times—and particularly of Northern France—was Philip of Valois, the first cousin of the king, Charles IV., who had just died.

Charles IV. had been the son of King Philip IV., and Philip of Valois was the son of Charles of Valois, Philip IV.'s brother. Philip of Valois was therefore the eldest in unbroken male descent of the house.

It might be claimed (and it was claimed by Edward III.) that the daughters of elder brothers and their issue should count before the sons of younger brothers. Now there were two female heiresses or their issue present as against Philip of Valois. Charles IV., the king just dead, had a sister Isabella, and Isabella was the mother of Edward III. of England.

But an elder brother to Charles IV., namely, Louis X., had himself left a daughter, who was now the Queen of Navarre.

If this principle that the daughter or the issue of the daughter of an elder brother should count before the male issue of a younger brother had been granted in its entirety, Edward would have had no claim, because this elder brother of Charles IV., Louis X., had had issue—that daughter, Joan, the wife of the King of Navarre. So Edward qualified this first general principle, that one could inherit through women, by another principle, to wit, that, though the *claim* to the throne should proceed through the *daughters* of *elder* brothers rather than through the *sons* of *younger* ones, yet the *throne* could *itself* only actually be held by a male!

By this tortuous combination Edward III. advanced his claim. His mother had been the grand-daughter of Philip III. of France, and he was a male. Her father was the elder brother of Philip of Valois' father, so he claimed before Philip of Valois.

The whole scheme is apparent from the following table:—

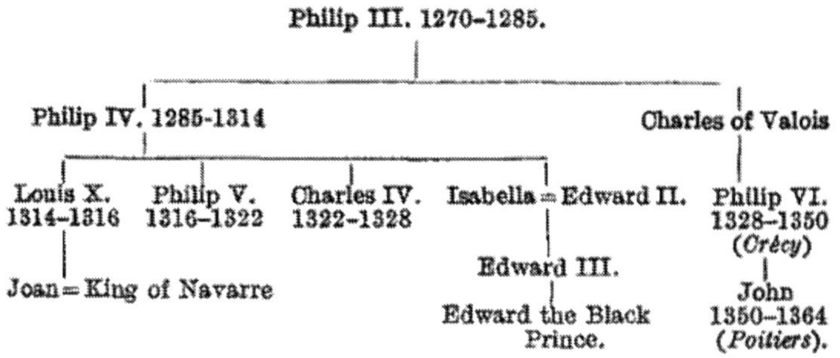

But, I repeat, we must not take Edward's political claim too seriously. His real object was not so much to establish himself upon the throne of France and to create a great French-speaking united monarchy of French and British under the single rule of the Plantagenets, as to try a great adventure and to see what would come of it.

It was this that gave to Edward's wars the character not of campaigns with a fixed object, but Great Raids, the very successes of which were unexpected and only half fruitful. It was this, again, which made him so uncertain and vacillating as to how he should use those successes when they came; which made him suggest now this, now that basis for peace after each victory, but never to insist very particularly, however surprising and thorough his work in the field, upon the French throne.

It was this, again, which gave to the actual results of his battles haphazard consequences, as it were, the most notable and permanent of which was the English hold upon Calais. And it was this which always left so huge a disproportion between the object he in theory desired to obtain and the forces with which he set out to attain it. To sum up, we shall only understand the victory of Crécy and the succeeding twin victory of Poitiers ten years later, if we conceive of the whole business as something of a tournament rather than a true political or even dynastic struggle.

Further, we must always remember that the leaders upon both sides came of one society, were of one speech and of one manner, often closely related in blood. We must remember that it was no desertion for a French lord to serve the King of England, and that even brothers would be found (as were the two Harcourts) honourably attached, according to the ideas of the time, to opposing forces.

Beneath this social aspect of the wars there was, of course, the growing national sentiment of the French and of the English. Most of the men who fought against Edward at Crécy, especially of the obscure men, thought of Paris as the only possible seat of authority, and of the Valois as their only possible king. All the Archers at Crécy, and many of the squires there—and a good half even of the forces at Poitiers—were English-speaking, and had no experience of life save that confined to this island, up to the moment when they set out for the Great Raids upon the Continent.

As the Hundred Years' War proceeded, as it approached its second phase in which Henry V. was actually successful in obtaining the Crown of France, or rather the reversion of it, the national feeling was growing rapidly upon either side, and by the time of Joan of Arc's campaign and of the subsequent loss of Normandy by the Plantagenets, everyone outside the small governing class of either country had come to think of the business as a national one upon either side. But with Crécy it was not so, and we must approach the military problems of Crécy with the political provision in mind that the whole affair of that battle and of its immediate successors was a feudal occupation—one had almost said pastime—engaged within the circle of that widespread French-speaking nobility, common to and intermarried between Gaul and Britain, which, for three hundred years, ruled society from the Grampians to the Mediterranean.

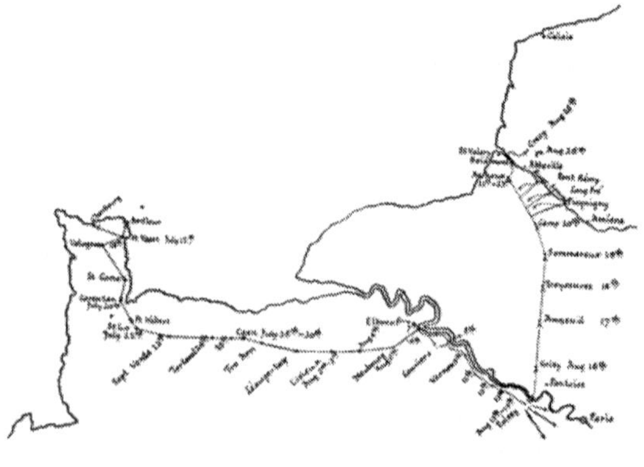

Larger Image

II THE CAMPAIGN OF CRÉCY

The Campaign of Crécy took place within a district of France contained by an east and west base 200 miles in length and an eastern border north and south 160 miles in length, and sketched in the map opposite.

The rectangular parallelogram so formed is nearly equally divided between land and sea, the south-eastern half being a portion of Northern France, and the north-western half the English Channel. The land half is thus roughly triangular, having Paris at its extreme south-eastern corner, Calais at its extreme north-eastern, the neighbourhood of Avranches with St Malo Bay at its south-western corner. It includes part of the provinces of Normandy, the Ile de France, Picardy and Artois, and part, or all, of the modern departments of the Manche, Orne, Calvados, Eure, Seine-et-Oise, Seine, Seine-Inférieure, Oise, Somme, and Pas-de-Calais.

It will be seen that this territory is nearly evenly divided by the River Seine, and the campaign of Crécy is also divided by that river in the sense that the English advance took place wholly to the west of it, and the English retreat wholly to the east of it.

The campaign, as a whole, resolves itself (up to and including the Battle of Crécy, which is the subject of this book, and excluding the continuation of the march after Crécy, and the capture of Calais) into an advance from the Channel coast to Paris, and a retreat from Paris to the Channel again, the two portions being divided by the crossing of the Seine at Poissy. The advance leaves the coast at the summit of that projection of Normandy called the Cotentin, and proceeds a little south of east towards Paris, the walls of which are reached by its outermost skirmishers, while the main army crosses the Seine at Poissy. The retreat is effected from Poissy northward to the victorious field of Crécy, and later from Crécy, on the same line, to the siege and capture of Calais.

The time occupied from the day of landing to the day of the Battle of Crécy inclusive, is but forty-six days, of which not quite two-thirds are taken up by advance, and rather more than a third by the retreat. The English troops landed on Wednesday, July 12th, 1346. They crossed the Seine at Poissy upon August 14th. They fought at Crécy upon Saturday, August 26th.

The total distance traversed by the main body in these two limbs of the campaign is instructive as showing the leisure of the first part, its advance, and the precipitancy of the second part, its retreat.

The distance by road as the army marched from St Vaast, where it landed, across the river at Poissy, and so to Crécy, was a total of 345 miles. Of this the first part, or advance, was 215, the second part, or retreat, 130. The first part occupied, counting the day of landing and the day of crossing at Poissy, not less than 34 days, while the latter portion or retreat of 130 miles, including the day of battle itself, took up not more than 12 days, or, excluding the battle, only 11. The average rate of the advance was not more than 6¼ miles a day, the average rate of the retreat very nearly double.

It must not be imagined, of course, that the advance took place in prompt and regular fashion. It was, as we shall see, irresolute for many days, and irregular throughout, while the retreat was a hurried one upon all but one day of which the troops were pressed to their uttermost. But the contrast is sufficient to show the difference between the frames of mind in which Edward III. took up the somewhat hazy plan of an "invasion," which was really no more than a raid, and that in which he attempted to extricate himself from the consequences of his original vagueness of intent. In the first, he was as slow as he was uncertain; in the second, he was as precipitate as he was determined.

In the last days of June, 1346, Edward III. had gathered a force, small indeed for the purpose which he seems to have had in mind, but large under the conditions of transport which he could command. It was probably just under 20,000 actual fighting men. At this point, however, as it is of material interest to the rest of the story, we must pause to consider what these units meant. When we say a little less (or it may have been a little more) than 20,000 fighting men, we mean that the "men-at-arms" (that is, fully equipped, mounted men, for the most part gentlemen), together with not 4000 Welsh and Border Infantry, and approximately 10,000 Archers, bring us near to that total.

But an army of the fourteenth century was accompanied by a number of servants, at least equal to its mounted armed gentry: men who saw to the equipment and service of the knights. No man at arms was fit to pass through a campaign without at least one aide, if only for armouring; and for all the doubtfulness of the records, we know that the Yeoman Archers were also served by men who carried a portion of their equipment, and who saw to their supply in action. It is impossible to make any computation at all accurate of the extra rations this organisation involved, nor of what proportion of these uncounted units could be used in the fighting. We are perhaps safe in saying that the total number who landed were not double the fighting men actually counted, and that Edward's whole force certainly was much more than 20,000 but almost as certainly not 40,000 men. We must imagine, all told, perhaps 5000 horses to have been assembled with the force for transport over sea: others would be seized for transport on the march. It is remarkable that Edward carefully organised certain small auxiliary bodies, smiths, artificers, etc., and took with him five cannon.[1]

It was not until Tuesday, the 11th of July, that the very large fleet which the King had pressed for the service was able to sail from the Solent and Spithead. It crossed in the night with a northerly breeze, and appeared upon the following morning off St Vaast.

St Vaast lies in a little recess of the north-eastern coast of the Cotentin, protected from all winds blowing from the outer Channel, and only open to such seas as can be raised in the estuary of the Seine by a south-easterly breeze. It was therefore, seeing the direction of the wind under which they had sailed, upon a calm shore that this considerable expedition disembarked. We may presume, under such circumstances, that though Edward had announced his decision of sailing for *southern* France, the point of disembarkation had been carefully settled, and that a course had been laid for it.

A small force composed of local levies had been raised to resist the landing. It was able to effect nothing, and was easily dispersed by a body of the invaders under the Earl of Salisbury, to whom that duty had been assigned.[2]

For nearly a week the army rested where it had landed, sending out detachments to pillage. Barfleur was sacked, Cherbourg was attacked, and the countryside was ravaged.

It was upon Tuesday, July the 18th, that the main body set out upon its march to the south and east.

No considerable body could meet them for weeks, and all the French Feudal Force was engaged near Paris or to south of it, and would take weeks to concentrate northward. Edward was free to raid.

The attempt to construct an accurate time-table of the march which Edward III. took through Normandy during his advance up the Seine as far as Poissy, and thence northward in retreat towards Picardy and the sea, has only recently been attempted.

Froissart, that vivid and picturesque writer who, both from his volume and his style, was long taken as the sole general authority for this war, is hopeless for the purpose of constructing a map or of setting down accurate military details. He had but the vaguest idea of how the march of an army should be organised, and he was profoundly indifferent to geography. He added to or subtracted from numbers with childlike simplicity, and in the honourable motive of pleasing his readers or patrons.

When, quite in the last few years, an attempt at accuracy in the plotting out of this march was first made, it was based upon not Froissart's but contemporary records, and of these by far the most important are Baker's *Chronicle* and the Accounts of the Kitchen, which happen to have been saved.

Baker's *Chronicle* was finally edited by Professor Maunde Thompson in

1889. The work is a standard work and generally regarded as the best example of its kind. In making his notes upon that document, Professor Maunde Thompson compared the halting-places given by Baker and other authorities with those of the Accounts of the Kitchen, and established for the first time something like an exact record. But many apparent discrepancies still remained and several puzzling anomalies. I have attempted in what follows to reconstruct the whole accurately, and I think I have done so up to and including the passage of the Somme from Boismont, a point not hitherto established.

First, I would point out that of all the few bases of evidence from which we can work, that of the Clerk of the Kitchen's accounts is by far the most valuable.

It should be a canon in all historical work that the unconscious witness is the most trustworthy.

I mean by "unconscious" evidence the evidence afforded by one who is not interested in the type of action which one is attempting to establish. Suppose, for instance, you wanted to know on exactly what day a Prime Minister of England left London for Paris upon some important mission. His biographer who sets out to write an interesting political life and to insist upon certain motives in him, will say it is the 20th of June, because Lady So-and-So mentions it in her diary, and because he finds a letter written by the Prime Minister in Paris on the 21st. Perhaps it is more important to the picturesqueness of the detail that the journey should be a hurried one, and without knowing it the biographer is biased in that direction. There may be twenty documents from the pens of people concerned with affairs of State which would lead us to *infer* that he left London on the 20th, and perhaps only five that would lead us to infer that he left on an earlier day, and, weighing the position and responsibility of the witnesses, the biographer will decide for the twenty.

But if we come across a postcard written from Calais by the Prime Minister's valet to a fellow servant at home asking for the Prime Minister's overcoat to be sent on, and if he mentions the weather which we find to correspond to the date, the 19th, and if further we have the postmark of the 19th on the postcard, then we can be absolutely certain that the majority of the fuller accounts were wrong, and that the Prime Minister crossed not on the 20th but on the 19th, for we have a converging set of independent witnesses none of whom have any reason to make the journey seem later than it was, all concerned with trivial duties, and each unconscious of the effect upon history of their evidence. It would be extraordinary if the servant had forged a date, and if we suppose him to have made a mistake, we are corrected by the equally trivial points of the postmark and the French stamp and the mention of the weather.

So it is with this manuscript record of the King's Kitchen expenses and of the several halting-places at which they were incurred. Wherever there is conflict, it must override all other evidence.

The Clerk of the Kitchen, to whom we owe this very valuable testimony, was one William of Retford. His accounts were kept in a beautifully neat, but not very legible, fourteenth-century hand, upon long sheets of parchment, and are now luckily preserved for our inspection at the Record Office.

With every day's halt the place where victuals were bought for the King, that is, where the King's household lay, has its name marked upon these accounts; but unfortunately the abbreviations used in the MS., coupled with the difficulty of distinguishing the short strokes [*e.g.* *m* from *ni*, *n* from *u*, etc.] upon parchment which time has faded, and on the top of that the indifference of the scribe to the foreign names themselves, do not render the task particularly easy. The MS. has not, I believe, ever been published. I have spent a good deal of time over it, and I will give my conclusions as best I can.

The main army stayed at St Vaast, as I have said, for six days, that is, until Tuesday, July 18th, 1346. This was presumably done to recruit the horses and the men. Foraging parties went out in the interval, but the bulk of the force did not move.

On that Tuesday it struck inland for Valognes, a march of 10½ miles. No proper coast-road existed even as late as the eighteenth century, let alone in the Middle Ages, and an army making for Paris or for the crossing of the Seine could not choose but to go thus slightly out of its way.

From Valognes there is a two days' march to Carentan, which town was the lowest crossing-place of the River Douves. We may naturally expect the halt between the two to have been about midway, and this would give us a town called Ste Mère l'Eglise, but the Clerk of the Kitchen puts down St Come du Mont. We conclude, therefore, that the King's staff did not follow the great road which had existed from Roman times, but went by bypaths to the east of it where St Come du Mont lies. It was a long day's march of over fourteen miles, but the next day's march, that of Thursday the 20th, to Carentan was a short one of not more than eight or nine (allowing in both cases for the windings of the side-road). On Friday the 21st the King lay at Pont Hébert. This is another example of something very like a long march followed by a short one upon the morrow. St Lô was the halting-place of the Saturday, and Pont Hébert is but four miles from St Lô. Of a total, therefore, of nearly seventeen miles, over thirteen are covered upon one day, and but four upon the next.

At this point it is worth noticing the character of all the advance with which we are dealing. Edward had been blamed for sluggishness. He was not so much sluggish as apparently without plan. He did not know quite what he was going to do next. His general intention seems to have been to make sooner or later for his allies in Flanders, and meanwhile to take rich towns and loot them, and to bring pressure upon the King of France by ravaging distant and populous territories which the French army could not rapidly reach. He therefore often makes a good and steady marching in this advance, but he also lingers uselessly at towns, and intercalates very short marches between the long ones. Thus he deliberately struck inland to St Lô on his way to Caen, because St Lô was a fine fat booty, instead of making by the short road which runs from Carentan through Bayeux. The whole character of the advance clearly betrays the point I have already made, that this early part of the Hundred Years' War was essentially a series of raids.

At this stage it is well to point out to the reader two difficulties which have confused historians. The first is the fact that the Clerk of the Kitchen often takes a shot at a French name which he has either heard inaccurately or which he attempts to spell phonetically, so that we have to interpret him not infrequently to make sense of his record.

The second is the fact that the chronicler will give some particular spot quite consonant with the marching powers of troops for one day, but different from that given by the Clerk of the Kitchen.

This apparent discrepancy is due to the fact that an army marches if it can upon parallel roads involving various halting-places for various sections of it on the same night. An army upon a raid such as this also throws out foraging parties and detachments, which leave its main body for the purposes of observation or of plunder.

Again, we must always regard the King's household (and therefore the Kitchen Accounts) as moving with what may be called "the staff." Often, therefore, it will go much faster than the rest of the army, while at other times it will lie behind or to one side of it. Thus, at the very end of this campaign you have a transference of the King's quarters, twenty miles to the north in one day, which would be a terribly long march for the army as a whole, and which, as a fact, we can discover on other evidence the army as a whole did not take.

With so much said, we can proceed to build up an exact account of the advance and the retreat.

Upon Sunday the 23rd of August Edward advanced from St Lô to a place which the Clerk of the Kitchen calls "Sevances." The spelling is inaccurate. The place intended is *Sept Vents*, twelve miles to the south and east of St Lô. But other portions of the army halted elsewhere in the neighbourhood, as we know from Baker. The next halt, that of the 24th, is at Torteval, only five miles away, but a portion of the army got south of Fontenay le Pesnel, which the King did not reach till the 25th, and which the Clerk calls "Funtenay Paynel." Three days are thus taken between St Lô and Caen, and the whole army arrives before the latter large town, the capital of West Normandy, upon Wednesday, July 26th.

The town of Caen was not properly defended. It had no regular walls, and was a very rich prey indeed. The Constable of France and the Chamberlain were in the town, and the castle was held by a handful (300) of Genoese mercenaries. There was an armed force of militia and of knights in the streets of the town, of what exact size we do not know. The Prince of Wales with the advance guard occupied the outskirts of the city which lie beyond the branches of the Orne (the northern branch now runs mainly in sewers under the streets from the Hôtel de Ville to the Church of St Peter). There was sharp fighting at the bridge, at one moment of which the King ordered a retreat, but the Earl of Warwick disobeyed the order. The King followed him, and the bridge was taken. There was considerable slaughter in the streets of the city; the Constable and the Chamberlain were taken prisoners, and about one hundred of the wounded knights. The English loss, which was not heavy, fell mainly upon the Archers and Spearmen, and the total, including wounded, was but five hundred, and was mainly due to the resistance of the inhabitants of the houses. The town was given over to pillage, and Edward thought of burning it, but was restrained. It is characteristic of the march that a delay of four days from the morning of the 5th was occupied in the loot of Caen, from which town (in communication with the sea by its river) Edward sent back his plunder on board the Fleet which he dismissed.

The army marched out of Caen on Monday, the 31st of July, and undertook its three days' march to Lisieux, the next rich town upon this random advance, now deprived of support from the sea. Edward probably intended to force some passage of the Seine, preferably, it may be surmised, at Rouen, or a little higher up, with the vague object of making for the north-east and Calais. We are not certain of this. It is more than possible that the capture of Calais later on in the campaign gave rise to the story that some such plan was intended. Anyhow, we get two halts and three marches between Caen and Lisieux, a distance of only twenty-five miles, which could easily have been accomplished in two days had there been a really definite plan in the commander's head. We may be pretty certain that there was not.

The halts of the King himself on the 31st of July and the 1st of August were made at two places which read in the MS. as "Treward," and an abbreviated name which stands for "Leopurtuis." The first of these is Troarn at the crossing of the Dives river. Other forces halted on that night at Agences, four miles to the south. The second is Léaupartie, a mile or so from Rumenise, where one other column halted, while a second column camped about five miles to the south. Lisieux was entered upon the 2nd of August after a march of ten miles on the part of the King, and of eleven and twelve on the part of the other two bodies.

At Lisieux two Cardinals who were despatched to offer terms met King Edward and proposed this arrangement to complete the war: that he should have the Duchy of Aquitaine upon the same tenure as his ancestors had held it. He refused those terms, and, after wasting a day at Lisieux, continued his march eastward.

Leaving Lisieux on the morning of the 4th, he pitched his tent that evening at Duramelle, a march of nine miles, with at least one column a mile ahead at Le Teil. On Saturday the 5th he got something better out of his troops, or at any rate out of the vanguard, and made something like seventeen miles to Neubourg.

I confess here to a very considerable doubt. The entry in the Accounts of the Kitchen is hopelessly misspelt, but the "Lineubourg" does not correspond to any other possible place, and Le Neubourg would be a very convenient halting-place for the King himself, well provisioned and lodged. We cannot believe, of course, that the army covered the full distance, but there is no reason why the King and his household should not have pushed on ahead with mounted troops. What makes it more probable is that the King spent the whole day of Sunday the 6th at Le Neubourg, presumably for the bulk of the army to come up and make two days' march of the twenty odd miles which the most distant contingents had to cover.

It was on the next day, Monday the 7th, that he reached the Seine, and approached that river, as we may presume, with the object of crossing it. It was a ten-mile march, and the whole force could be on the banks before evening at Elbœuf.[3] But the bridges were broken and it was impossible. It was from this point of Elbœuf that the raid turned to follow the valley of the Seine up towards Paris, always seeking some crossing-place, and always finding the bridges broken. The nearer he got to Paris the more dangerous became Edward's position, and the larger grew the forces of the French King in the neighbourhood of the capital which threatened him.

Tuesday the 8th was spent in ravaging the country. Pont de L'Arche was burnt in revenge for the destruction of its bridge; a detachment went round by Louviers, which was looted, but the King himself went forward by the river bank and lodged that night at Vaudreuil, ten miles on from Elbœuf (which the Clerk of the Kitchen calls "Pount-Vadreel").[4] The bulk of the force halted at Léry, a mile or two behind.

Upon Wednesday, August 9th, Edward lay at Angreville[5] (the "Langville" of the accounts), just south of Gaillon, and on Thursday the 10th, having burnt Vernon, where *again* he found the bridge cut, at Jeufose, rather more than eleven miles march up the river. ("Frevose," as I read it in the MS.) His next hope for a bridge was at Mantes, and he was getting perilously near the heart of the country and the gathering French forces. That bridge was nine or ten miles along the road. He found it cut like all the others.

He was already across the borders of Normandy, and anxiety must have been growing upon him. He seized Mantes after some resistance. It was useless to his purpose, and he hurried on another six miles to Epone ("Appone" in the Accounts), making that day a really long march in his natural haste and compelling his escort to the same—sixteen miles. But he both fatigued his main army in that attempt, and it also lost some time in storming a fortified house on "the White Rock,"[6] because the next day he evidently had to wait for stragglers to come up, advancing but a couple of miles to Aubergenville,[7] where we find him upon Saturday the 12th. Upon the 13th, the Sunday, he got his opportunity. A march of only eight miles[8] brought the host to

Poissy, and there, though the bridge was cut, the stone piles upon which its trestles had stood were uninjured. Edward at once began to take advantage of this and to put his artificers to work. All that Sunday and all the Monday the task proceeded, and during this delay parties were despatched to ravage. They burnt St Germain and St Cloud. An advance party entered the Bois de Boulogne. But there could, of course, be no thought of an attack on Paris with so small a force and without base or provision.

By Tuesday the 15th of August these ravaging parties were recalled, and the whole host was streaming across the repaired bridge at Poissy.

This day, Tuesday the 15th, is strategically the turning point of the campaign. In an attempt to note in history no more than the great raid of Edward up to the very walls of the Capital, and his rapid and successful retreat, the crossing of Poissy would form the central term of our story. As it happened, however, the great chance which occurred to Edward in that retreat upon the field of Crécy, and his magnificent use of it, has eclipsed the earlier story, and for many the interest of the campaign as a whole, and the importance of this rapid seizure and repair of Poissy, is missed.

While his army was crossing the river, Edward received the challenge of the King of France. It was native indeed to the time: a sort of tournament-challenge, offering the English monarch battle upon any one of five days, in that great plain between Paris and St Germains which the last siege of the French capital has rendered famous in military history. The French feudal levies for which Philip had been waiting were now fast gathering, especially those for which he had had to wait longest, the main forces which had been away down south in Guienne. Edward most wisely refused the challenge, for it would have been against great odds, and to accept, though consonant to the spirit of the time, would have been a ludicrously unmilitary proceeding. In place of such acceptation he sent back false news that he would meet Philip far to the south. He then proceeded to cross the river and make the best haste he could back northwards to the sea. The French King found out the trick; a day and a half late he started in pursuit with his large and increasing host. That host was gathered at St Denis when on the Wednesday night, the 16th, Edward had got his men to Grisy, well north of Pontoise, and something like seventeen miles by cross roads from his hastily repaired bridge across the Seine. What followed was a fine feat of marching.

On the next day, the 17th, he had got his forces more than another seventeen miles north and had camped them by Auneuil. In two more days, by the evening of Saturday the 19th, they were yet twenty-five miles further north as the crow flies (and more like thirty by the roads), at Sommereux. Edward halted at Troussures (of which the clerk makes "Trusserux") to see it file by, and on the morrow, Sunday, August the 20th, he was at Camps in the upland above Moliens Vidame, another push of fifteen miles for mass of the force, and of more than twenty for himself and his staff.

At this point came the crux of his danger. All during that tremendous feat of marching (and what it meant anyone who has covered close on fifty miles in three days under military conditions will know—there are few such) the great host of Philip was pounding at his heels.

Now, if the reader will glance at the map at the beginning of this section, he will see that just as Edward had been under a necessity to cross the Seine in the first part of his raid, he was now under a still greater necessity of crossing the Somme. A force much larger than his own was pressing him against that river into a sort of corner, and his only chance of safety lay in reaching the Straits of Dover through the county of Ponthieu, which lay beyond the stream. Every effort had been made to press the march. The force appears to have been divided for this purpose and to have marched in parallel columns, and the single case of marauding (the burning of the Abbey of St Lucien outside Beauvais) had been punished with the death of twenty men.

To turn and meet his pursuers (who were evidently in contact with him through their scouts) would have meant, so long as he was on this side of the Somme, no chance of retreat in case of defeat.

Every mile he went to the north the Somme valley, already a broad expanse of marsh upon his flank, grew broader and more difficult. The decision, therefore, which Edward took at this critical moment, at once perilous and masterly, showed that rapid grasp of a situation which, for all his lack of a general plan during this campaign, this great soldier could boast. In the first place, he himself rides forward no less than twenty full miles to the village of Acheux. He has behind him the whole army strung out in separate bodies parallel to the Somme. Himself, from the head of that long line of twenty miles, commands all that should be done along it. He next orders separate bodies to approach the valley and seek a crossing, first, if possible, up river, then, as they fail, lower and lower down, and each to be ready as it is foiled at each bridge to fall back north in concentration, and to group in gathering numbers further and further down the stream, and near to his place at the head of the line, Acheux.

The whole thing is a fine piece of sudden decision, and is at once a combination of the rapidity of the retreat and of the attempt to force the river, in this the fourth week of August 1346, which so nearly brought disaster to the English force.

Three days, the 21st, 22nd, and 23rd, were taken up in this manœuvre. The English flung themselves successively against the bridges: Picquigny, Long Pré, Pont Rémy. The hardest and first push was at Picquigny at the beginning or southernmost of the effort. The body detached for that effort was beaten back.

It was the same with the next blow lower down at Long Pré: the same lower down still at Pont Rémy. At no bridge were the English successful. Everywhere the valley was impassable to them, and as they attempted one place after another down the stream with its broadening marshland and now tidal water, to find a traverse seemed impossible.

At last, then, upon Wednesday the 23rd of August the whole host was gathered, foiled, round its King at Acheux. He marched on a few miles to Boismont, going on his way through Mons, and there, as it chanced, picking up a prisoner who proved invaluable: for that prisoner betrayed the ford.

As the English army lay at Boismont that night of the 23rd, the broad estuary of the Somme stretched to the north of them with no more bridges across it, cut or uncut, and apparently no fate but a choice between a desperate action against superior numbers (nor any retreat open) and surrender.

Edward's only chance lay in the discovery across that mile of land (flooded at high tide, and at low tide a morass) of some kind of ford. Such a ford existed. With difficulty, but in the nick of time, it was discovered and used; the French force defending it upon the further side was overthrown, and the retreat and its dependent victory of Crécy were made possible.

Edward had had good faith that "God and Our Lady, and St George would find him a passage," and a passage he found.

The crossing of that ford and the advance to Crécy field must form the matter of our next section, "The Preliminaries of the Action."

The reader will note that in the latter part of the above I have wholly abandoned the more usual account of the last three days of the retreat from Poissy to the Somme, and that the reconstruction I have attempted includes several matters hitherto not suggested in any recent history, and is in contradiction with the view which has hitherto been most generally accepted.

The evidence upon which I rely for this description of the retreat on Acheux and subsequently on Boismont will I hope be found set out in detail in the number of the *English Historical Review* for October 1912. Meanwhile, I owe it to my readers, who may use this book for purposes of school or university work, to state briefly the way in which the matter has hitherto been set forth, and my reason for adopting this new version.

Most Froissart MSS., which have misled history in this regard, say that King Edward was at *Oisemont* upon the evening of the 23rd. Lingard, the father of all modern English historical writing, and a man whom every historian begins by reading (though very few go on by acknowledging him), expanded this mere reference into a whole phrase, and wrote that Edward "had the good fortune to capture the town of Oisemont, and so find a night's lodging." A neglect of military conditions, or of the map, or of both, has perpetuated the error. Edward was never at Oisemont. The argument against it, and in favour of *Boismont*, is dependent upon a number of converging proofs, which I will very briefly recapitulate.

(1) The MSS. of Froissart are none of them original.

(2) They vary among themselves with regard to this particular word, most of them giving "Oisemont," but one giving "Nysemont."

(3) Even where all the MSS. agree with regard to a place, and where Froissart certainly mentioned it, he is wildly inaccurate, evidently going by

hearsay, and often by a doubtful memory: thus he has no idea on which side of the Seine the town of Gisors stands, and he calls the village of Fontaine a "strong town," etc.

(4) Even were he an accurate, he is not a contemporary authority. He had to depend entirely upon older accounts which we can prove that he misread, or did not read at all, but only heard spoken of, and very often botched horribly.

(5) In this particular campaign he is particularly haphazard. Thus, upon the all-important point of the order in which the various crossings of the Somme were attempted, he gets them at sixes and sevens, describing the first last and the last first. He was a man always attending to picturesqueness of incident, and one who thought exactitude very negligible.

Those are the five points which weaken any positive evidence which Froissart may give. But it is the evidence independent of Froissart, and of his accuracy or inaccuracy, which is so overwhelming.

(1) Oisemont lies actually ten miles *back* from Abbeville upon the line of the retreat. To occupy Oisemont was to incur a deliberate running into that danger which it was all Edward's effort to avoid.

(2) We know, as a matter of fact, that Philip, the King of France, was before the night of the 23rd abreast of Abbeville; a retreat upon Oisemont would therefore have been physically impossible to Edward.

(3) Oisemont would have involved keeping in touch with bodies ten, twelve, fifteen, and twenty miles distant, even if Oisemont had been occupied for two days, whereas the only mention we have of that occupation represents it as taking place on the 23rd.

These three points render it, as to two of them morally impossible, as to one of them physically, that Edward could have been at Oisemont upon that night. But they are negative: we have positive points which clinch the whole matter. These are:—

(1) Edward marched with his *whole* army to the ford or it could not all have crossed, therefore it was concentrated before he marched. The march was a very short one. Even Froissart says that "he started at the break of day" and reached the ford "a little after sunrise." It must also have been short because we know as a matter of positive history that the soldiers who took that morning march waited some time for the tide to ebb, *then* fought a sharp and successful action upon the northern bank of the river, and again on the same day stormed certainly one and possibly two defended places: also that their total march before the night, and beyond the river, was quite ten miles, including the actions just mentioned.

(2) We also know that there was an assault on St Valery, which was actually *twenty* miles from Oisemont by the nearest roads!

(3) We know that the traitor was captured at Mons, which, if Edward had been at Oisemont, would have meant that someone had not only caught him at that great distance from Oisemont, but had brought him back (a total ride of twenty-four miles) without previous knowledge that he was capable of the

valuable information he only gave later and after offers.

(4) There is no contemporary mention of Oisemont, but we do positively know from contemporary evidence that the King's household was, and had been for three days, at Acheux.

Now all this combined is quite conclusive. Oisemont is impossible. Boismont satisfies every part of the evidence. An hour's riding from it permits the attack on St Valery. Mons, where the traitor comes from, is only two miles off; the march from Boismont to the Ford is just such an advance as would take the dawn and sunrise of a day—whereas the advance from Oisemont, impossible for all those other reasons, would involve fourteen to fifteen miles of marching, and is utterly incompatible with the idea of two or possibly three heavy fights, and the long march succeeding it.

One last piece of evidence would be conclusive even if we had not all the rest. There is contemporary record of the Mayor of Abbeville watching from the heights of Caubert Hill the English army streaming northward to concentrate round the advanced position of the King. From that height such an advance could be discerned crossing the plateau which leads to Acheux, to Mons, and to Boismont. You could no more see a concentration on Oisemont from it than you could see a concentration on Greenwich from Camden Hill.

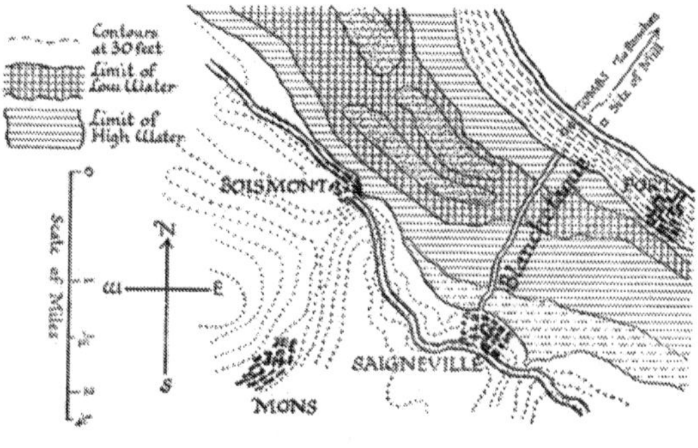

Larger Image
Sketch showing Estuary of the Somme at Blanchetaque in 1346

III THE PRELIMINARIES OF THE BATTLE

The manœuvres of the French and English armies preliminary to the Battle of Crécy are so instructive upon many points, involved movements so hazardous and so complex, gave rise to so sharp a series of engagements, and form in general so large a part of our subject, that they merit a far larger study than do the approaches to most battles.

They illustrate the comparative lack of thought-out plan which characterised medieval warfare; they afford a contrast between the compact and fairly well organised command of Edward III., and the chaotic host of the King of France. They show the effect upon the military profession of a time without maps and without any properly managed system of intelligence; and, above all, they show the overwhelming part which chance plays in all armed conflict between forces of the same civilisation and approximately the same aptitudes.

The situation upon Wednesday the 23rd of August (at which point we concluded the survey of Edward III.'s great raid through Normandy, and of his retreat down the line of the Somme) is already known to the reader, and will be the clearer if he will look at the map upon page 28.

Edward had made a very fine march indeed, not only averaging something like twelve miles a day, or more, but arranging for expeditions to leave the main host during the latter part of this rapid retreat, and attempt to force, at various points, the passages of the River Somme. We have seen that he was compelled, if possible, to force a passage because he would otherwise find himself shut up between the Somme and the sea, with a much superior force cutting him off to the south. In case of defeat he would have no line of retreat, and even in case of success, unless that success were overwhelming, he would find himself strategically stalemated, still caught in a trap, and still doomed to await the next onslaught of the enemy. We have further seen that with every mile that he proceeded towards the sea his ability to cross the Somme decreased. The river runs through a marshy valley which, even to-day, is a mass of ponds and water meadows, and which then was a belt of marsh. It is bounded on either side by fairly steep banks, rising to heights of 60, 70, and 100 feet, and inland to 150, between which the flat swamped land grows broader and broader as one approaches the sea. At Picquigny this level belt of swamp through which the Somme twines is quite 500 yards across. At Long Pré it is nearer 800, below Abbeville it is 1000, and at the point whence Edward overlooked it when he was halted at bay on the evening of that 23rd of August, it is well over 2000 yards in width and nearer 2500.

Boismont, a village climbing the southern bank of the estuary, was the spot on which the King had gathered the army upon the evening of that Wednesday, and, not a day's march behind him, the most advanced mounted men of his pursuers, with the King of France among them, were camping. The peril was extreme, and an issue from that peril as extremely doubtful.

It was hopeless for the army to attempt to retrace its steps to the upper river. To have done so would have been to march with the flank of its march exposed to an immediate advance of French forces, and almost certainly to be caught in column; and Edward had already suffered such repulses before Long Pré, Pont Rémy, and Picquigny as left him no hope for success should he attempt these bridges again. His only chance was to find, if it were possible, some practicable ford across the broad estuary itself that lay before him.

The moon was within a few hours of the full that night, the highest of the spring-tides was making—in the open sea they were at their full height of 25 feet, an hour before midnight,—and though where he would strike the estuary he might hope for a tide more tardy, Edward had before him as he watched, his only avenue of escape, a great flood that appeared to deny him all access to the further shore.

Every effort was made to discover from local knowledge whether any passage existed. The highest rewards were offered, in vain, for in all that countryside a feeling which if not national was at least strongly opposed to the invader, forbade treason, and the near presence of the French King's great force was an active reminder of the punishment that would attend it. Late in this period of suspense a guide was found.

A man of the name of Gobin Agache, who had been taken prisoner by the army, was that guide. His was that "invaluable" capture which I mentioned in the last section. He was a peasant of those parts, and a native of Mons-en-Vimieux, through which the army had marched from Acheux to Boismont. He yielded to temptation when all others had refused. He was promised a hundred pieces of gold (say £500 of our money), his own liberty, and that of twenty of his companions. For that price he sold himself, and promised to discover to the King and to his army the only practicable ford across the estuary.

Just at the end of the night the host set out and marched during the first hours of the moonlit Wednesday morning along the old road which still leads over the hills that separate Boismont from Saigneville and marked the southern bank of the valley. The marshalling was long; the full ordering of the force, now that it was all gathered together and marching along one narrow way, inexpeditious; and the two miles that separated the head of its column from the neighbouring village were not traversed by its last units, nor was the whole body drawn up at the foot of the hills against the water until the sun of that late August day was beginning to rise, and to show more clearly the great sheet of flood-water and the steep distant bank beyond it.

The place to which their guide had led them was the entry to the ford of Blanchetaque, a name famous in the military history of this country. Hidden beneath the waters which, though now ebbing strongly, were still far too deep for any attempt at a crossing, ran the causeway. By it, upon the faith of the traitor, they could trust to gaining the opposite shore. As the racing ebb lowered more and more, the landward approaches of that causeway appeared in a lengthening white belt pointing right across towards the further bank, and assured them that they had not been betrayed. It was built of firm marl in the midst of that grassy slime which marks the edges of the Somme valley, and they had but to wait for low water to be certain that they could make the passage. Beyond, upon the northern shore which showed in a high, black band (for it was steep) against the broadening day, they could distinguish a force that had been gathered to oppose them.

It was mid-morning before the ebb was at its lowest,[9] and they could begin to march "twelve abreast, and with the water no more than knee-high," across the dwindled stream now at its lowermost of slack water, and running near the further bank with a breadth not a fifth of what it had been at the flood. But before proceeding further and describing the assault shore, I would lay before my readers the process by which I have established the exact locality of this famous ford. It has been a matter of considerable historical debate. It is and will always remain a matter of high historical interest, and this must be my excuse for digressing upon the evidence which, I think it will be admitted, finally establishes the exact trajectory of Blanchetaque.

The site of Blanchetaque is one which nature and art have combined to render obscure: nature, because a ford when its purpose disappears and it is no longer kept up, that is, an artificial ford, tends to disappear more rapidly than any other monument; art, because the old estuary of the Somme has of recent years been further and further reclaimed. It was, when I first began studying this district, already banked across below Boismont, and, if I am not mistaken, the great railway bridge right across the very mouth of the river has, in the last few months, been made the boundary of the reclaimed land.

Now, Blanchetaque was an artificial ford. We know this because there is no marl formation near by, and could be none forming a narrow rib across the deep alluvial mud of the estuary; the marl, then, can only have been brought from some little distance. It is not only an artificial hardening which we have to deal with, but one in the midst of a tidal estuary where a violent current swept the work for centuries. Finally, the cause for keeping the ford in some sort of repair early disappeared in modern times before the process of reclaiming the land of the estuary began. Numerous modern bridges, coupled with the great development of modern roads, permitted the crossing of the Somme at and below Abbeville: notably the Bridge of Cambron. The railway, the growth of the tonnage of steamers, and other causes, led to the decline of the little riverside town of Port—formerly the secure head of marine navigation upon the river and largely the cause that Blanchetaque was kept in repair.

Again, the reclamation of the land has been carried out with a French thoroughness only too successful in destroying the contours of the old river bed. In the sketch map on p. 60 I have indicated to the best of my ability the channel of the river at low tide as it appears to have been before reclamation began, but even this can barely be traced upon the levelled, heightened, and now fruitful pastures.

It is all this which has made the exact emplacement of Blanchetaque so difficult to ascertain, and has led to the controversies upon its site.

Now, if we will proceed to gather all forms of evidence, we shall find that they converge upon one particular line of trajectory which in the end we can regard as completely established.

We have in the first place (and most valuable of all, of course) tradition. Local traditions luckily carefully gathered as late as 1840,[10] but the indications of the peasants pointing out the traditional site of the then ruined way were, unfortunately, not marked on a map. What *was* done was to give an indication unfortunately not too precise, and to leave it on record that the northern end of the ford was "from 1200 to 1500 metres below Port." This gives us a margin of possible error, not of 300 yards as might be supposed, but of more than double that distance, for Port itself is 500 yards in length from east to west. We can be certain, however, that so far as tradition goes we need not look more than a mile below Port for the ford, nor less than say half a mile from its last houses.

Fortunately, we have other convergent indications which can guide us with greater precision.

We must remember that, apart from the bringing of merchandise over to the neighbourhood of Port, the ford, which may, and most probably did, exist before Port became of any importance, led all the central traffic of the Vimieux country (which is the district on the left bank of the Somme) towards the Straits of Dover and their principal port at Boulogne.

Now, the way from the right bank of the Somme to Boulogne is interrupted by several streams, much the most marshy and broad of which is the Authie. The Romans bridged the Authie at *Ad Pontes* in the course of their great Trunk Road to Britain, and any way which led from the lowest ford over the Somme to Boulogne would have to join that great Trunk Road before or at the bridge if it were to take advantage, as commerce would have to do, of that sole passage of the very difficult and marshy Authie valley which can nowhere be crossed save upon a causeway. I have in a former page remarked upon the importance of Ad Pontes (the modern Ponches), and pointed out that it gives the whole county its name of Ponthieu. We must expect, therefore, any direct commercial way northward from the ford to make directly for Ponches. To strike the great Trunk Road higher up would be to go out of one's way; to strike it lower down would be to strike the Authie Valley at an impassable point.

When an ancient way has disappeared, certain indications of its track, especially as that track may be presumed to be direct, survive, and among these are wayside tombs, parish boundaries, and mills or other places which, for the conveyance of heavy merchandise, are placed near such a road if possible. All these three kinds of indications are available in this particular case. The medieval mill which was so important a monopoly of the medieval community was not built in the most natural place for it, on the summit of the hill just above Port, but some thousand yards and more away down the river bank, and over against it is a group of tombs. Moreover, between the two runs the long north-western boundary of the parish or commune of Port which is prolonged in the boundary of the parish of Sailly.[11] We have here, then, a convergence of proof which confirms the vaguer traditional site, for the end of this line upon the river, passing between the tombs and the old mill, strikes the bank within the limits of distance from Port which were set down in the local notes printed in 1840.

But there is more. The forming of successive embankments one below the other for the gradual reclamation of land in the Somme estuary was not an easy matter. They had to be strong to withstand a strong tide, and there was no good bottom to be found in the deep mud of the valley floor. It is a significant evidence of this difficulty that the embankments stand so far apart, and that the last has had to take advantage of the long-established work of the railway viaduct. It is therefore a legitimate conjecture that the hard bottom afforded by the old Blanchetaque would be made use of, and as a fact we find the principal embankment between Port and the sea coinciding exactly with the line established by the tombs, the parish boundaries, and the site of the mill.

There is even more than this. If we follow the present embankment across the estuary towards the southern bank, we find ourselves checked before reaching that bank by the now canalised and artificial straight ditch of the Somme. There is no bridge, but on the further side leading across the remaining 700 yards to the southern bank, a village road exactly continues the direction, and this road, older than the reclamation of the valley, is the last converging point clinching the argument.

It cannot be doubted that the road leading from Saigneville northward across the flat to the canal, and continued beyond the canal by the embankment, is the line of the old Blanchetaque.[12]

Though the French army had been pursuing Edward during his march upon the left bank of the Somme, the possibility of his getting across the estuary had not been neglected, and a force had been detached to watch the right bank at the point where the only passage across the stream, Blanchetaque, touched that right bank.

Here one of Philip's nobles, Godemard de Fay, was waiting with a considerable force to oppose the passage. The exact size of this force is not easy to determine, for it is variously stated, even by contemporary authorities, but we are fairly safe if we reckon it at more than 2000 and less than 4000 men, some hundreds of whom were mounted knights. In other words, it counted in "capital units" from one-sixth to one-eighth of Edward's army, and, counting all fighting men against all fighting men, perhaps much the same proportion. There was sharp fighting, but it was defeated, principally through the action of the Archers. In Godemard's command was a very considerable body of Genoese cross-bowmen. As we shall see when we come to the Battle of Crécy itself, this arm was gravely inferior in rapidity of fire, and possibly in range, to the English long-bow. The latter weapon could deliver three to the cross-bow's one, and to this, coupled with the discipline of the English column, the success must be ascribed. Grave as was the balance of numbers against the French side, equal armament and equal discipline should have enabled it to prevail. The holding of a *tête de pont* with a smaller number properly deployed should always be possible against a larger column compelled to debouch from a narrow line, especially a line of such difficulty as a ford across a broad stream.

The action was a picturesque one, and the sight presented to a spectator watching it from the heights behind Godemard's command must have been a picture vivid and well framed. One hundred mounted and armoured knights, carefully chosen, led the way across the ford. They were met actually in the water itself by mounted men advancing on to the causeway from Godemard's side, and the twin banners of Edward's two marshals and the cries of "God and St George!" with which the English vanguard met the enemy rose for a few moments from a confused mêlée of men and horses struggling in the stream. But the issue was decided by the comparative strength of missile weapons, and not by the sword. The Genoese cross-bowmen behind the French knights, and upon either side of their rear, shot into the English mounted ranks with some success, when the Archers of Edward, who were just behind the knights, and seem to have deployed somewhat over the marshy land on either side of the ford, returned their fire with that superiority of the long-bow which helped to decide this campaign. It was the regular fire of the Archers, the weight and the rapidity of it, which finally threw the supporting infantry of the French command into confusion, and permitted the mounted head of the English column to force its way over the landward end of the ford and through the now isolated body of French knights. Once the bank was gained, the English head of the column in its turn held the *tête de pont*, and the passage of the whole force was only a question of time.

But time was a factor of vast importance at this juncture: how important what immediately followed will show. A force of anything between twenty-four and thirty-nine thousand men, combatant and non-combatant, with its wagons and sumpter horses, the considerable booty of its raid, its tents, its reserve of armour and of weapons, we cannot reckon, even upon a front of twelve deep, at less than a couple of miles in length, even under the best and strictest conditions of marshalling. Indeed, that estimate is far too low and mechanical. It is more likely that by the time the head of the column was pouring from the causeway on to the right bank of the estuary, and there deploying, a good third of the armed men were still waiting upon the further shore to file over the narrow passage.

At any rate, before the great bulk of the train could have got upon the ford, the first horse of the King of France's scouts and vanguard appeared upon the sky-line of the heights above Saigneville, and immediately a considerable force of the enemy were upon the English wagons with their insufficient rearguard. The King of France himself, following upon Edward's track mile by mile, had reached Mons, had learnt that Edward had doubled back from Boismont, and had detached a body to cut across country to the ford on the chance of preventing Edward from crossing. He had not been quick enough to achieve this, but the French appeared in time, as I have said, to catch the wheeled vehicles behind the English army before they had got into line upon the causeway. Edward, with that good military head, which always seized immediate things upon a field, had stayed somewhat to the rear of the main body to watch for such an accident. He was not able to save the bulk of his train, but he saved his army. Much of the booty and of the provision fell to the French.

This mishap, which shows how close a chance permitted the safety of Edward's fighting force, had no little effect upon the succeeding two days, for it left the English army in part without food. I say "in part," because for some of them the defect was remedied, as we shall see, by the capture of Crotoy.

So the English army passed with the loss of some of its train, but with very little loss of men. Pursuit was impossible; the tide now rising forbade even the thought of it, and somewhere about noon the entire host was marshalled upon the northern bank of the river, and was safe. The whole story forms one of the most striking details in the history of medieval warfare.

What followed the discomfiture of Godemard's command and Edward's passage with his forces intact, is not easy to gather in the authorities themselves, though it is easy enough to reconstruct with the aid of the Kitchen Accounts, and by the help of the analogy of Edward's action throughout the campaign. The King's tent, his domesticity, and what we may by an anachronism call his staff, proceeded to the edge of the forest of Crécy, which lies upon the inland heights north-eastward of the ford, a distance of five miles.

But it did not proceed there directly. In company with the whole army, it first turned north-westward down the bank of the estuary to the capture of the castle and town of Noyelles, rather more than two miles away. This castle it took, and it is characteristic of these wars that the mistress of it was English in sympathy, and, what is more, had married her daughter to the nephew of one of Edward's principal generals. From Noyelles on the same day, Thursday, Edward and the staff turned back north-eastward towards the forest. There was a skirmish at Sailly Bray with Godemard's command, which, though defeated, was not yet broken, and which had hung upon the flanks of the English army. But the belated struggle was of little importance, and Edward camped that night upon the edge of the forest in the neighbourhood of Forêt L'Abbye to the west of the little railway line and station which mark those fields to-day.

Meanwhile, during the remaining hours of that Thursday, the customary raiding and pillaging parties which had been characteristic of all this great raid were being sent out. The chief one under Hugh the Dispenser took Crotoy and thus provisioned his own force and perhaps some of the neighbouring detachments, but the bulk of Edward's army "went famished that day," and, for that matter, were insufficiently provided during the ensuing Friday as well.

The host camped upon that Thursday night somewhat widely spread around its King, with foraging parties still distant and appointed to return upon the morrow.

Upon that morrow, the Friday, the advance north-eastward was continued. It was organised in a fashion whose exactitude and forethought are worthy of note, considering the haphazard conditions of most medieval fighting, and of Edward's own previous conduct of the earlier part of this campaign.

These were the conditions before him: he must get as best he might to the Straits of Dover, that is, up northward and north-eastward, and he may already have had a design upon Calais.[13] The force which was pursuing him had been checked by the tide of the Somme. It was too large to use Blanchetaque with any rapidity. He knew that it must double back to Abbeville in order to cross the river before it could turn northward again and come up with him. From where it lay, or rather where its commander and staff had lain, between Mons and Saigneville, that morning and noon, back to Abbeville was a matter of seven or eight miles; a distance nearly as great separated him from Abbeville upon his side. He had gained a full day even if the French army had been collected, highly disciplined, and in column. Instead of that it was scattered over twenty miles of country. Many of its contingents were still following up, and it was under very various and loose commands. Even should a large body of French appear upon the next day, Friday, Edward had the forest at hand with which to cover his troops long before contact could be established. But good scouting informed Edward that there was no chance of such contact, at least before Saturday. The whole of the next day, Friday, would be at his disposal to bring his troops where he would, and he proposed to get them on the far side of the forest, that is, in the neighbourhood of Crécy town, during the interval.

Whether he had already decided on that Thursday to make a stand we cannot tell, but it is not probable, because he had as yet no knowledge of the positions beyond the forest, and of the chance the ground would afford him of meeting an attack. One thing he already knew, which was that his retreat was secure. The pace of the French pursuit might compel him to a decision on Saturday at earliest, but, short of complete disaster, he had a road open behind him across the Authie by the passage of Ponches and along the great Roman way which led from Picardy to the Straits of Dover.

What he did was this. He sent the bulk of the army round by the main road whose terminals are Abbeville and Hesdin, and which skirts the forest. His own household he accompanied through the wood, presumably with the object of keeping in touch with the foraging parties who would during that Friday be coming up along the southern edge of the woods to follow the main force along the high road. A further advantage of so moving through the wood himself was that he could thus lie upon the flank of his force and let it march round him until it got in front of him in the open country by Crécy. Then he could join it, coming up in its rear, that is, upon the side from which attack was expected, gather his information, study the positions, learn the approach of the French advance, and in general organise the coming action, if an action should prove necessary. Edward camped, therefore, in the forest upon that Friday night, and upon the further side of it, just above Crécy town; while the whole of his main body was marching up to the right or east of him by the high road that skirts the woods. That main force, joined by the foraging parties which had gone further westward on the day before, easily covered the few miles, and camped on the evening of the Friday upon the ridge which runs in a level line eastward and northward from just above the town of Crécy to the village of Wadicourt, for somewhat over a mile. Leaving his tents and domestics upon the edge of the wood, he spent the last hours of that day establishing his forces along the ridge for the night, for it was there that he had now determined to await the French army and to bring it to action.

The advantage of that position which upon emerging from the forest Edward had immediately seized, will be dealt with in the ensuing section; meanwhile we must return to inquire what was happening to the French pursuit.

We must not consider the French army as one united body. Had it been that, it would not have been defeated, and, what is more, the particular place of Crécy in military history, and its lesson of the contrast between the older feudal and the newer regular levies, would never have been taken; for Crécy, as we shall see, was largely a victory of things then new over things then old. No records give us precisely the positions, number, or routes of the King of France and his allies, but we know the following points, from which we can construct a general picture.

First: The commands were various and disunited. That personal system which had arisen five hundred years before, and more, when the old Roman tradition of the Frankish monarchy gradually transformed itself into a series of summonses to lords who should bring their vassals, was still the method by which a French host was tardily and irregularly summoned. For general and lengthy expeditions it was sufficient. For the prosecution of the innumerable local conflicts of the Middle Ages it was actually necessary. Upon occasion at long distances from home, and after long companionship in the field, if there were also present a very leading character among the feudal superiors, and especially if that character were clothed with titular rank, it could achieve something like unity of command. But Philip's army, the last contingents of which were still in act of joining him, enjoyed no such advantages. At least five separate great bodies, four of which were largely subdivided, were loosely aggregated over miles of country, gathering as they went chance reinforcements, and losing by chance defections.

Secondly: A certain proportion of regular paid men, including the foreign mercenaries, accompanied the King of France. These were in part with the King himself, in part detached to watch the passages of the river.

Thirdly: The King, with a considerable personal force, and with some of his mercenaries as well, was up in the neighbourhood of Saigneville upon the noon and early afternoon of the Thursday. He retraced his steps towards Abbeville, and recrossed the river there himself either upon the Thursday evening, or more probably upon the Friday.

Fourthly: Round about Abbeville the bulk of the incongruous force was gathered when the King reached it, and very considerable bodies lay in the suburbs to the north of the town.

Finally, we know that on the Saturday morning the King heard Mass and took Communion at the Church of St Stephen (now demolished).

From all this we can construct a fairly accurate view of the French advance, especially when we consider where the French forces lay when they reached the field. From Abbeville to the field of Crécy is, as the crow flies, ten miles. A great main road (along the further part of which the English had marched on the Friday) led to the neighbourhood of the field and past it: the main road which goes from Abbeville to Hesdin. By this road, breaking up probably rather late upon the Saturday morning, the largest of the loosely gathered French contingents marched. Far to the right of them over the countryside would be advancing the other feudal levies under the King of Bohemia and John of Luxembourg, the exiled Count of Flanders, the ex-King of Majorca, and other friends, connections, and vassals whom Philip had summoned with their arrays. It is to be presumed that certain bodies on the extreme right went up by the Roman road which misses Abbeville coming from the south, and makes for Ponches, bounding the battlefield of Crécy on its extreme eastern side.

Following this chaotic advance of the dispersed host, gathered in a jumble, the wholly untrained peasant levies which had been swept up from the villages on the advance proceeded in disorder. And it was thus without regular formation, save among the Genoese mercenaries (some 15,000 in number at the outset of the campaign, though we do not know of what strength on the field itself), that the first lines of mounted men caught sight from the heights of Noyelles[14] and Domvast of the English line on the ridge of Crécy three miles away.

It was early in the afternoon before that sight was seen. The wind was from the sea, and gathering clouds promising a storm were coming up before it, and hiding the sun.

Before these advance lines of the French army, and between it and Edward's command, the ground fell gradually away in low, very gentle slopes of open field towards the shallow depression above which a somewhat steeper and shorter bank defended the line, a mile and a half long, upon which Edward had stretched his men.

There was an attempt at some sort of deployment, and the first of three main commands or "battles" were more or less formed under Alençon, the French King's brother. Immediately before it were deployed the trained mercenaries, including the Italian cross-bowmen under their own leaders, Dorio and Grimaldi. Behind was a confused mass of arriving horse and foot, the King himself to the rear of it, and much of it German and Flemish separate commands. We do not know their composition at all. Still further to the rear, and stretched out for miles to the south, straggling up from Abbeville, came, that late afternoon, the rest of the ill-ordered host at random. Before the action was begun, the whole sky was darkened by the approaching storm, and violent pelting rain fell upon either host. The clouds passed, the sky cleared again, but it was nearly five o'clock before the first attack was ordered.

In order to explain what followed we must next grasp the nature of the terrain, and the value of the defensive position upon which Edward had determined to stand.

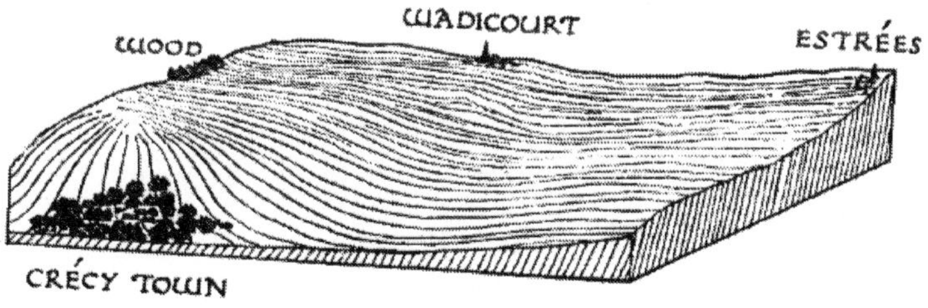

IV THE TERRAIN OF CRÉCY

The action decided upon the field of Crécy developed wholly within the central space shown in the frontispiece of this volume.

The general frame within which the battle took place must be regarded as a parallelogram corresponding to the exterior limits of that map, not quite four miles in length from east to west, and some 2½ miles in breadth from north to south, having the town of Crécy a little to the north of the medial line, and a good deal on the left or western side of the area. But the emplacement of the troops and the actual fighting, including the partial pursuit by the victors, is wholly contained within a smaller area, which lies aslant, with its major axis pointing north-west, its minor axis pointing north-east, and surrounding the dip called "the Val aux Clercs."

The aspect of this countryside is that of so many in the north-east of France. The passage of six and a half centuries has not greatly modified it. The limits of the Royal Forest of Crécy are what they have been perhaps from Roman, certainly from early medieval, times. The characteristic hedgeless, rolling, ploughed land, which is the normal landscape of all French provinces and of many others, has been disturbed by no growth of modern industrialism, and its contours remain unmodified by any considerable excavations of the soil. The villages attaching to the battlefield, Estrées, Wadicourt, Fontaine, are in extent, and even in appearance, much what they were when the armies of the fourteenth century occupied them, and the little market-town of Crécy has not appreciably extended its limits.

Even minor features such as the small groups of woodland and the spinnies seem, judged by our remaining descriptions of the battle, to be much the same to-day as they were then.

The terrain of Crécy offers, therefore, an excellent opportunity for the reconstruction of the medieval scene, and I will attempt to bring it before the eyes of my readers.

Ponthieu is a district of low, open, and slightly undulating fertile lands, whose highest ridges touch such contours as 300 feet above the sea, and the depressions in which, very broad and easy, do not commonly fall more than a 100 feet or so below the higher rolls of land. In the particular case of the field of Crécy we shall have to deal with figures even less marked. The crests from which the opposing armies viewed each other before the action average full 200 feet above the sea; the broad, shallow depression between its confronting ridges descends to little more than sixty feet below them.

All this wide expanse of fertile land, affording from one lift of its undulations and another great even views for miles and miles, is cut by streams which run parallel to each other in trenches five to seven miles apart, and make their way by curiously straight courses north-westward to the neighbouring sea. These are the Conche, the Authie (the crossing of whose marshes by the great Roman road formed those *pontes* which, as we have seen, give the district its name of Ponthieu), and the Maye.

This last little river alone concerns us. We deal in the matter of the Battle of Crécy only with the first rising waters of the Maye. Its source springs just below the village which derives from that river-head its name of Fontaine, and the Church of Crécy stands not two miles down the young stream. These two miles of its course, and a slight depression tributary to this its upper basin, mould the battlefield.

For this shallow depression, called the "Val aux Clercs," among the least of the many long waves and troughs of land upon which Ponthieu is modelled, was the centre of the engagement, and, though too short and shallow to develop the smaller stream, such water as it collects is tributary to the Maye. This depression runs up from the level exactly north-eastward, gradually rising until it fades, not quite two miles above the river, into the upper levels of the plateau.

On either side of this Val aux Clercs lift the soft and inconspicuous slopes that bound it. The one that bounds it on the north and west, and from which a man faces the south-east and the direction of Amiens, was the eminence occupied by the army of Edward III. At its southern end, where it overlooks the narrow rivulet of the Maye, it descends abruptly to the meadow level of the stream. The fall at this terminal of the bank is one of 100 feet. Its slope varies from one in ten to one in twelve, and on that slope and on the meadow level below it the little town of Crécy stands. There is the mouth of the Val aux Clercs, and the further one walks along the road which marks the position of the English line, and the nearer one approaches Wadicourt, the shallower and less conspicuous and flatter does the Val aux Clercs appear upon one's right, as its depression rises towards the general level of the plateau. At last, in the neighbourhood of Wadicourt itself (the first houses of which stand 2000 yards from the last houses of Crécy) the depression has almost disappeared.

The bank or fall of land from this crest of the English position down to the lowest point of the trough, steeper towards its southern, or Crécy, easier towards its northern, or Wadicourt, end is, upon the average, a slope of one in thirty; just steep enough to produce its effect upon a charging crowd (especially over soil drenched by rain), and falling just sufficiently to give their maximum value to the arrow-shafts of the long-bow, which was the chief arm of Edward's command.

The opposing slope, that which lies to the south and east of the vale, and from which the traveller faces the sea-breeze blowing from a shore not fifteen miles away, is much easier and more gentle even than its counterpart. The ridge of it stands above the lowest point of the Val aux Clercs no higher than the corresponding and opposite ridge which the English King occupied with his army, but the fall covers double the distance. It is not 400 yards, but more like a mile, and the average of the decline is one in fifty at the most.

Moreover, this opposing ridge is neither as cleanly marked as the Crécy-Wadicourt line nor parallel to it. It is impossible to fix upon it, with any definition, a true crest. The slope undulates very gradually into the general level of the plateau, and is so formed that the Val aux Clercs is funnel-shaped, much wider at the mouth on the Maye than towards its upper end.

The depression, therefore, which was the theatre of the action, is in the main V-shaped, and its mouth is a full mile in breadth, while its last faint upper portion is not half that width.

Such, in detail, is the field of Crécy.

I have attempted in the cut opposite p. 91 to express graphically its main features as they would appear upon a model carved in wood and plotted to show the actual relief of the soil.

I will conclude by pointing out to the English reader a curious parallel. The field of Crécy has many analogies to the field of Waterloo. In both cases two opposing ridges roughly determine the general plan. In both a depression, double and complex in the modern, single in the medieval, instance, lies between the two lines. That of Crécy, as was suitable for a day in which no missiles of long range were available, is somewhat more marked and affords somewhat more of an obstacle to the offensive than that of Waterloo. In both the French formed the attacking force and in both the defensive position was chosen with singular mastery. Indeed, an eye for a defensive position marks Edward's plan most strongly, and is, quite apart from the successful result of his action, his best title to repute in military history.

At the close of this section the plainest duty of an historian, as well as the satisfaction of common humour, compels me to allude to a characteristic production of the University of Oxford. There has proceeded from this university a school-book, perhaps the most universally used in the public schools of this country, known as *Bright's History of England.* I was myself brought up on it. It is taken, I suppose (like much other Oxford matter), as something hall-marked and official. This text-book has upon page 226 of its first volume a full-page map of the Battle of Crécy. It is fair to say that such a production could not have proceeded, I do not say from any university upon the Continent of Europe, but from the humblest schoolmaster in a French, Swiss, or German village. The features marked upon it are wholly and unreservedly imaginary. There is not even the pretence of a remote similarity between this grotesque thing and the terrain of the famous battle: it is a pure invention. It is almost impossible to express in words the difference between this product of fancy, and even the most inaccurate map sketched from memory, or the merest jottings set down by someone who had no more to guide him than some vague recollection of an account of the battle. There is nothing in it bearing the remotest resemblance to any hill, river, road, wood, village, or point of the compass concerned with the field of Crécy, and to this astonishing abortion is modestly added in the left-hand bottom corner, "From Sprüner." I have not by me as I write Sprüner's collection of historical maps which were given us at the University, but if that eminent authority was the model for such a masterpiece, it is a sufficient commentary upon the rest of his work. I *have* before me as I write the flabbergasting plan in *Bright's History* which I have treasured ever since my boyhood, and I trust that this note may be read by many who still believe that the function of our universities is to train the governing class of the nation, not so much in learning as in "character."

Contrast the excellent and accurate little map in the first-rate manual which Mr Barnard published twelve years ago from the Clarendon Press. The whole of this book is to be most highly recommended. I believe that this map, the only doubtful features of which are the angular formation of the English Archers and the concentration of the French rear upon the Roman road, is from the pencil of Mr Oman.

V THE ACTION

King Edward, upon that Saturday morning before he had yet caught sight of the French, of whose advance his scouts informed him, rode on a little horse slowly up and down the ranks encouraging his army, as it sat and lay at rest, with shield and helm and bow upon the grass before each man, along the crest of the slight hill.

In his hand the King bore a white wand and no weapon, and this visitation of his lasted until nearly ten o'clock. His last orders were that all his men should eat and drink heartily, and he himself conveyed that order to his own division, which lay behind the main line. He had organised the defence upon a very simple pattern.

That battalion which was called the First Battalion consisted of 1200 men-at-arms, that is, fully armoured knights upon horseback, with 4000 Archers and 4000 Welshmen. They occupied that turn or shoulder of the slope which runs round from the town of Crécy itself into the beginning of the Val aux Clercs, and were under the nominal command of the lad the Prince of Wales. But at his side the real orderers of that force were Warwick and Oxford. Such was the English right.

Next, in the centre, and back from the first battalion, was the line of English Archers. It was very carefully organised, with the object of a purely defensive action. Small pits were dug before each man's station, and this infantry was arranged in "harrow" formation, much as trees are planted in an orchard in *quincunx*, so that any five of them formed a figure somewhat like the five in a pack of cards. It is evident that this formation, if the men were sufficiently dispersed, as they were, gave the freest play to their missiles, all of which could be shot through the intervals; and when we remember the rate of fire, three to one of the cross-bow, we shall understand how formidable was this infantry, and how well able it was to break any cavalry charge prepared by nothing more than the shots of the Genoese. All the tradition and sentiment of medieval warfare gave to the mounted knight the glory of battle, but, as I shall have occasion to remark in the sequel, the great feature of Crécy was the presence of an ordered, highly trained infantry, expected to await, and capable of awaiting, a rush of horse until that cavalry should receive at, say, fifty to eighty yards the whole weight of a furious and sustained discharge of missiles. Beyond the Archers, some 3000 in number at this point, were 1200 mounted knights, who, together with the Archers at the centre, were under the command of Northampton.

There may have been a certain number of Archers to the left again of these knights, but, at any rate, Northampton's command covered the rest of the ridge and reposed upon Wadicourt. Here, lest it should be turned, the left flank of the English line was protected by a park of wagons drawn up close together, vehicles taken from such of the train as had been saved from the French attack upon the rearguard at the ford two days before.

The remainder of the wagons, provisions, and impedimenta were drawn up in the rear near the wood, and in front of them and between them and the defensive line upon the ridge was a strong reserve of over 10,000 men under Edward himself. Taking no account of non-combatants, we must reckon Archers, armoured men and spear-men together at perhaps 25,000 men, and certainly not more than 30,000; but we must remember, as I said upon a former page, that every Archer was served by aides, that a man-at-arms needed a squire, and that drivers and domestics of various kinds, and many recruits from Normandy, swelled the host.

The large force against which this defensive was drawn up has been variously estimated. Its dispersion over the countryside, the lack of any cohesive command, the absence of all precise figures, the considerable bodies of wholly untrained country folk who were straggling up behind the army, make an estimate of the actual forces engaged on the French side extremely difficult. We do not know how many Germans, Luxemburgians, and others had been brought up with the feudal levy. The rough guess of contemporaries at the whole numbers present and arriving during this confused marshalling of Philip's host, calls it 100,000. A recent and very careful English authority has estimated the enemy actually in line at 60,000. If we say that Edward met forces more than double his own, but not three times his own, we are as near the truth as we can hope to get. But the right way to estimate the disproportion between the offensive and the defensive upon this famous day is to contrast the fully armoured mounted men of either side, and, further, to contrast

The trained infantry, armed with missile weapons.

The infantry, trained or untrained, armed only with spear, dagger, or sword.

Upon such an analysis we get some such result as follows:—

Some 4000 fully armoured mounted men in Edward's command, of whom only 3000 or less were out of the reserve and in the line. Some 7000 Archers actually in the defensive line, with a much smaller number (unknown) in the reserve. Add 4000 Spearmen, for the most part Welsh. Against these on the offensive you may set, at the very least, quite four times their number of fully mounted armoured men and probably six times their number, or even more.

As against the English Archers, we must count for the missile arm upon the French side somewhat less. The only contemporary authority, Villani, who gives us any exact figures, names 6000 as their number.

When we come to the few trained non-missile infantry of the English forces—some 4000 in the line, not counting the reserve,—and contrast them with the rabble of untrained and scattered French countrymen, most of whom were still coming up in the rear and did not take part in the action (save to suffer slaughter in the darkness after it was over), we can take any multiple we choose. They may have been five, six or eight times as numerous as the Welshmen with whom they did not come into contact at all.

It will be seen from the above that the real point of the battle, and that which decided it, was the power of the trained missile infantry of Edward (1) to await a charge of horse in no matter what numerical superiority it might arrive, confident that they could always check it before it reached their line or broke it; and inspired by that confidence, because (2) the only missile infantry that could be brought against them to prepare such a cavalry charge was armed with a weapon which delivered only one shot to their three. That was the deciding element of the Battle of Crécy: the power of the long-bow to stop horse upon any front equivalent to the front of the Archers, and the confidence of the bowman in that power.

The action opened regularly enough with the advance of the French missile infantry, the Genoese mercenaries, at the hour, as I have said, of about five o'clock. They proceeded down the slight slope into the Val aux Clercs, followed at a foot's pace by a strong body of the first battalion of the French mounted knights under Alençon.

Advancing thus deployed, a body of 6000 men had difficulty in keeping its line, a thing essential to the simultaneous effect of short-range weapons. Twice they were halted to correct their alignment, and though perhaps at the second halt they were at the lowest point of the valley and just in extreme range of the English arrows from the height above, those arrows did not yet come. The English had been ordered to reserve their fire. They began to climb the opposing slope, shouting as was their custom, and after a third halt had been called, and a third strict alignment made so near to the English front as to be certainly in range for their cross-bows, the order to shoot was given. With the first flight of the Genoese bolts, the English Archers took each man his step forward and began pouring in that terrible fire, sustained, accurate, and rapid, to which they were so admirably trained, and of which hitherto, save in the fight at the ford, no example had been given in continental warfare.

Under that murderous and unceasing rain of missiles the Italian mercenaries, whose weapon compelled them to a complicated process of winding and ratcheting and laying, very ill-suited to such a strain, fell into disorder. A sufficient proportion of them broke, and their confusion at once angered and churned up the great body of mounted French knights, which awaited impatiently immediately behind their line. They were ridden down in the eagerness of these armoured horsemen to retrieve this first check by a charge, and Alençon's men spurred hard (badly hampered by that obstacle of their own men fallen into confusion before them) upon the English right and the Prince of Wales's battalion. Some of them got home, especially those who found themselves opposite the most advanced section of the Prince of Wales's command, where it stood thrust forward in a semicircle upon the shoulder and last slopes of the hill. The boy himself was unhorsed, and for a moment the pressure was severe.[15] But the effect of the arrow fire upon all the rest of the charging line told heavily. It never got home. Indeed, it must have been apparent to Edward at that moment that for all the fixed tradition of chivalry and that overwhelming atmosphere of military religion which in every age, according to its traditions, confuses the soldier, had he kept all his men at arms in reserve and put Archers only in the front line, they would have sufficed to win his battle.

There stands upon the Crécy end of the ridge a great mound to this day. It is the foundation of an old stone windmill which stood there for centuries, and which has been shamefully pulled down within living memory. From that mill it was that Edward watched the whole action proceeding upon the slope beneath him. He saw the head of the French charge get home but its extended line wavering, checked, and broken up on the Val aux Clercs as a continuous rain of arrows poured in. He saw all the front ranks of horses broken: the animals lashing out or fallen stampeding rearward, mounted or riderless: the heavily armoured knights fallen helpless and trampled, the whole thing a vast confusion.

It was near six o'clock. The westering sun was within an hour of its setting, and shone right up the vale, coming aslant upon the burnished armour of the charge. Had this kind of warfare already established a tradition, and had men learned by experience what unshaken infantry could do against horse, it would already have been apparent that the action was decided. But there was no such experience and no such knowledge. Over the long slopes of open field which fronted the English ridge, line after line of knights were coming forward in successive waves, as though mere weight of horses and men could win home in spite of the increasing welter of flying, dead, and maddened mounts, and of fallen men and iron that now lined all the front with a belt of obstacle more formidable than earth or wall. And of those, such few as could struggle through to within range might hope to escape the deadly and now converging fire which struck horse after horse as the foot of the ridge was reached. By gaps in the deadly confusion of the stampede and the corpses, round to their right further and further up the valley (upon their left the marshes of the Maye forbade a turning movement), the French charges followed and spread. A dozen or more were counted, and each as it came met the missile defence and was broken, with no counter missile offensive to tame that fire.

The sun was setting, but one effort was made which should have been made far earlier in the short crisis. It was an effort of the French right to turn the English left by Wadicourt.

Due, we may imagine, to no regular order, an occasion seized upon by some one commander who saw his chance, a charge of horse was led right up to that end of the English line, the barricade of wagons prevented its getting home, and, though the struggle was violent, the obstacle was never pierced or overcome. Well after sunset, and as the light was fading, the King of France himself led a great body to the centre, and seems to have come into range of the arrows, but he, no more than any of his lieges, could force horse against steady infantry and an unremitting fire. The darkness came, the late moon rose, and still were desultory and sporadic charges continued, haphazard and blindly. They had not even a hazard of success. These last efforts of the failing battle were repelled with ease, but even up to midnight the final pulses of the fight throbbed, with lesser and lesser pulsations; until after these seven hours of it—most of it by darkness, and all the while the line of Archers standing unbroken, and all the while supplied with their unexhausted ammunition, and finding strength to draw and to discharge—the thing was over.

Throughout that night great bodies of disordered peasantry, half-armed, the militia of the Communes, fled or wandered aimlessly southward over the bare, rolling land. The mounted knights had ridden away from a field where all was utterly lost, and the English line broke up to move forward by the light of lanterns over the face of the countryside, to despatch or to capture the wounded, to loot, to search for the faces and the ensigns of the greater dead. But in that darkness the magnitude of the result was not seen. The English army seems to have guessed the issue mainly by the dying down of the noise, and the ceasing of the cries of men rallying to their lords' banners.

This was the end of the Battle of Crécy, in the night of Saturday the 26th of August, 1346.

Early upon the Sunday morning, Edward's forces stood to arms again, not knowing whether even yet a new attack might not be made. Mist covered all the landscape, through which fog, dimly, bodies of men seemed to be advancing upon them from the south. They were reinforcements of Philip's come up in ignorance of what had passed the day before, or at any rate not appreciating how decisive the day had been. Five hundred knights riding out easily dispersed them. Further bodies straggling up in similar fashion were dealt with in detail, and all that morning the English soldiers going at large over the fields found and put to the sword lost fragments of militia, came, as they tracked the flight, upon dead and wounded lords, and cut off bewildered remnants, making they knew not whither over the land.

The total French losses will never be known. The legend of disaster calls them now ten, now twenty thousand. Of the mounted and armoured men of rank the heralds made a precise account, and returned a list to King Edward of 1542 fallen and dead upon the front of the battle and in the first fields of the retreat. To these due sepulchre was given. The mass of the fallen were buried in common trenches, marks of which may be seen to this day; and it is said that fires were lit to rid the ground of the dead.

The English loss was wholly insignificant. Its exact amount, like that of its enemy, we cannot tell, because a list of but two knights, one squire, and forty of the rest, not counting a few Welsh, is all that we are given. But, even if this total (which hardly corresponds to the fierce mêlée at the beginning of the action on the right) be below the true number, we may be certain that that number was very small indeed. The line was never pierced; the English fight was wholly defensive, and a defensive maintained at range against troops which disposed, after the first rout of the Genoese, of no missiles upon their side.

Upon the Monday morning, the 28th of August, the host set forth upon its northern march, quite free now from any danger of pursuit. By the first days of September it had sat down before Calais. All winter and all the succeeding summer the blockade continued, and upon the 4th of August 1347, nearly a year after Crécy, the town was taken and the lasting fruit of that engagement was garnered. Calais remained an English bastion upon the Continent for more than two hundred years.

Footnotes:

[1] We have this upon the evidence of a contemporary, Villani. It has, of course, been denied by our modern academic authorities, but without evidence.

[2] The theatrical character which attaches to warfare through the fourteenth century appears at this very outset of the campaign. Edward knighted the Black Prince and sundry other commanders on a hill overlooking the fleet and the harbour just before the main body disembarked. The Black Prince had already been knighted, and the ceremony was mere parade.

[3] He did *not* go to Rouen, or near it, as the map in Mr Fortescue's work (vol. i. p. 37) presumes. Rouen was, he found, too strongly held. There is no time for the big loop of twenty miles which Mr Fortescue introduces, and no evidence for it.

[4] This is not N. D. de Vaudreuil, as Professor Thompson suggests, but St Cyr just beyond where the bridge is.

[5] This point has also proved puzzling. Thus Professor Thompson calls it "difficult to find." What the clerk heard and set down was the peasants' term "L'Angreville."

[6] This, as Professor Thompson rightly says, is not on the modern maps. It stood just above *Nezel* near the modern Chateau between that village and Falaise or "The Cliff."

[7] So I read the meaningless rigmarole of the Clerk of the Kitchen. But I may be wrong. Professor Thompson inclines to Ecquevilly, a mile or two further on.

[8] Or *six*, if we read Ecquevilly. The main army halted at Flins.

[9] The low tide after the full moon occurred on that 24th of August at about half past-six o'clock in the open sea and nearer eight o'clock in the

estuary, or even later; for we must allow quite seven hours' ebb to five hours' flow in that funnel in its old unreclaimed state.

[10] *Antiq. de Pic.*, vol. iii. pp. 131, etc.

[11] The parish boundaries are not absolutely straight, as, after the fashion of modern French communal boundaries, they follow the corners of the oblong strips of peasant cultivation, but the aggregate of straight lines, all in one continuous direction, marks a quite unmistakable trajectory.

[12] The traveller going by rail to-day from Paris to Calais or Boulogne, may note at the second station after Abbeville a wood upon the heights to his right, and upon his left the reclaimed valley of the Somme. The next station he passes is that of Port, with the church of the village upon his right as he leaves it, and the embankment which he sees crossing the valley floor upon his left, a mile further on, marks the passage by which Edward III. and his army forced the then broad estuary of the river.

[13] See p. 45.

[14] Not to be confounded with the other Noyelles upon the Somme, ten miles away.

[15] It was at this moment that news was brought to King Edward of his son's peril, and that he replied "Let the child win his spurs"—sending the messenger back empty, but having care immediately afterwards to despatch reinforcement.

www.ingramcontent.com/pod-product-compliance
Lightning Source LLC
Chambersburg PA
CBHW071716130725
29531CB00036B/1697
9781023181693